S0-DXM-430

A HOLY TIME OUT

t a parenting class a few years ago, many parents expressed frustration. One mom knew her children manipulated her, but she felt powerless and guilty about it. Another was tired of her kids' constant bickering. Still another told of her four-year-old screaming, "You're not my mom!" whenever they went out in public. Time and again, the instructor's response was, "Who is the adult here?" It gave us all pause, knowing our behavior needed to change if we wanted real peace. During Lent we ask ourselves the same question. Who is the adult? How do we calmly bear the responsibility of guiding our children to God's kingdom of goodness, joy, and peace? It's not easy, especially in a world that doesn't understand God's life within us. But Lent gives us an opportunity to stop and take a breather. Even if it's only a few minutes each day, finding God's presence in our families can make all the difference. This booklet can help. First, settle in with the excerpt from the daily Mass reading. Read the reflection. Say the simple prayer together with your family, and do the activity together. Sure, you're the parent here, but Jesus holds your hand at every moment.

TWENTY-THIRD PUBLICATIONS A Division of Bayard; One Montauk Avenue, Suite 200, New London, CT 06320; (860) 437-3012 or (800) 321-0411; www.23rdpublications.com

ISBN: 978-1-62785-133-6

Copyright ©2016 Connie Clark. All rights reserved. No part of this publication may be reproduced in any manner without prior written permission of the publisher. Write to the Permissions Editor.
Printed in the U.S.A.

JOEL 2:12–18 » 2 CORINTHIANS 5:20—6:2 » MATTHEW 6:1–6, 16–18

WORLDS COLLIDING

Even now, says the LORD, return to me with your whole heart,
with fasting, and weeping, and mourning. JOEL 2:12

"Something's in my eye," my son insists, getting off the bus after a week at science camp. I pretend not to see the tears he tries to hide. Every mom knows that children often can't understand their own overwhelming feelings, especially when they're caught between conflicting worlds of friends and family. Adults too can find ourselves overwhelmed by the Father's unconditional love. We just can't believe anyone could be so gracious, merciful, slow to anger, and rich in kindness with us. We return to God during these days. It's okay to let the tears flow.

FAMILY PRAYER *(Based on today's first reading, Joel 2:12–18)*

Parent: Lord God, we gather here in your presence.

   All: God, you are kind and good.

Parent: Today we begin our time of fasting, prayer,
   and service to others.

   All: God, you are kind and good.

Parent: Help us be like you: kind, good, and rich in mercy.

   All: God, you are kind and good. Amen.

Spend a moment in silence, thinking of ways God has been good
to you this year.

FAMILY ACTIVITY

Today, the Holy Father sends out priests as "missionaries of mercy" to share and model God's love, kindness, and mercy. Make your family "missionaries of mercy" by deciding how each of you will share love, kindness, and mercy this Lent.

Deuteronomy 30:15–20 » Luke 9:22–25

LIFESAVER

*"For whoever wishes to save his life will lose it,
but whoever loses his life for my sake will save it."* Luke 9:24

Of course I want to save my life. I have a responsibility to be around for my children. So how do Jesus' words apply to parents? Focusing on our family is every parent's job, but when we see ourselves as little islands disconnected from the world, we may be surviving, but we're not living. Jesus' way of selfless service helps us really live. When I help out in my child's classroom or work as a team mom, is it so that my kids will get more attention? Does it all just feed my own family? Is there another way to selflessly serve someone? Lent is a time to think about this.

FAMILY PRAYER

Parent: Our Lady of Lourdes, you appeared in a cave to a girl
         named Bernadette.
   All: We pray for the sick.
Parent: You are kind and good. You are mom to all of us.
   All: We pray for the sick.
Parent: Bring all sick people to your Son, who heals
         in the Father's name.
   All: We pray for the sick. Amen.

Pray for people you know who are sick right now.

FAMILY ACTIVITY

Today is World Day of the Sick and the Feast of Our Lady of Lourdes. Have kids draw or color a picture of Mary to share with someone who is ill.

3

ISAIAH 58:1–9A » MATTHEW 9:14–15

FAST CONNECTION

Lo, on your fast day you carry out your own pursuits, and drive all your laborers. Yes, your fast ends in quarreling and fighting.

ISAIAH 58:3–4

For years I fasted on Ash Wednesday and Good Friday because it was what you were supposed to do. But my fast days were full of my own pursuits. I really didn't see the connection to love. And love—not rules—is the whole point of fasting. I see Jesus suffering on the cross because he loves me and my family so much. I can give up a full meal (as long as I'm physically able) as a small return for this love. My kids can keep Jesus' love in mind as they perform some small sacrifice. This is the way we say, "Yes, Lord, we love you."

FAMILY PRAYER

Parent: Good Jesus, do we love you?

    All: Yes, Lord, we love you. Yes!

Parent: Jesus, we'll show our love by saying "yes" when you ask us to love our neighbor.

    All: Yes, Lord, we love you. Yes!

Parent: Help us remember every day how much you love us.

    All: Yes, Lord, we love you. Yes! Amen.

Talk about ways we can show our love for Jesus.

FAMILY ACTIVITY

On paper or poster board, write the word "YES" in large letters. Have everyone write or draw things they will do in Lent to answer Jesus' call to love.

Isaiah 58:9b–14 » Luke 5:27–32

STAY CLOSE

Jesus saw a tax collector named Levi sitting at the customs post. He said to him, "Follow me." Luke 5:27

"I don't have any business here," she said tearfully. Attending a meeting of eucharistic ministers at my parish, this anguished mom asked to be excused from serving on certain Sundays when she cared for her elderly mother. "I get so angry and impatient," she sobbed afterwards. "I shouldn't be allowed near Jesus on those days." The beating she gave herself was heartbreaking to witness. We are all tax collectors and sinners. Please don't ever let yourself get talked into the idea that you are so "bad" that you should stay away from God. Jesus loves you. He wants you in his presence today.

FAMILY PRAYER

Parent: Jesus, sometimes we've felt broken and in pain.
   All: To you, O Lord, I lift up my soul.
Parent: Good Jesus, you are with us in all these moments.
   All: To you, O Lord, I lift up my soul.
Parent: Help us remember those moments so we can
        help others who suffer.
   All: To you, O Lord, I lift up my soul. Amen.

Ask if anyone noticed someone who was in pain today.

FAMILY ACTIVITY

Create a special place in your home where anyone can go when they're in need of God's comfort or help. Make it a comfortable spot, with a crucifix, candle, holy books, and other reminders of God's love.

Deuteronomy 26:4–10 » Romans 10:8–13 » Luke 4:1–13

SERVICE REMINDER

*"You shall worship the Lord, your God,
and him alone shall you serve."* Luke 4:8

I sometimes forget to exercise and eat right, but little reminders help me stay on track: a framed picture of my family hiking together, a calorie-counting app on my phone. Then I ask myself, why do we have problems with little reminders about following God? We can't see God physically, so a crucifix on the wall, some good spiritual reading, or a set daily prayer time are some ways we remind ourselves that he is with us always. He is our most important goal. What reminders can you use during Lent to help your family stay on the right track toward God's kingdom?

FAMILY PRAYER

Parent: Lord, teach us your ways. Open our hearts to your great love for us; help us hear your voice.

All: Your ways, O Lord, are love and truth.

Parent: Lord, we get off track sometimes. Lead us back to the path that leads to you.

All: Your ways, O Lord, are love and truth. Amen.

Talk about the ways of love and truth in your family's life.

FAMILY ACTIVITY

Make valentines for Jesus. Cut cross and heart shapes from paper, and have family members write or draw ways they will love Jesus this month. Display your valentines as love reminders for your family.

LEVITICUS 19:1–2, 11–18 » MATTHEW 25:31–46

ONE FOR ALL

"For I was hungry and you gave me food, I was thirsty and you gave me drink, a stranger and you welcomed me." MATTHEW 25:35

Pope Francis has said he wants a church that is both poor and for the poor. Since families are domestic churches, what if each of us decided that our family is "for the poor"? Or the disabled? The unborn? The homeless? Orphans? Victims of war? What group needs the help and patronage of your domestic church? Whom can your family pray for and actively help? Pray about this today and see where God leads you. Then make a plan to act with your family on behalf of this group during these forty days.

FAMILY PRAYER

Parent: Jesus, when you are hungry, we'll give you food.
    All: Jesus, you are there in everyone we meet.
Parent: When you are thirsty, we'll give you something to drink.
    All: Jesus, you are there in everyone we meet.
Parent: When you need clothing and shelter,
        we'll share what we have.
    All: Jesus, you are there in everyone we meet. Amen.

Talk about what it means to see Jesus in each person.

FAMILY ACTIVITY

The Corporal Works of Mercy come from today's gospel. Read Matthew 25:31–46 with your kids to help you decide whom your family will care for during Lent.

Isaiah 55:10–11 » Matthew 6:7–15

SAVING OUR CHILDREN

"And forgive us our trespasses, as we forgive those who trespass against us..." Matthew 6:12

I was eight years old when my brother died in a car accident caused by a drunk driver. My brother's widow chose not to pursue legal action, and I'll never forget my mom's answer when I asked why: "That wouldn't bring Bob back, would it?" To this day, I've never tried to learn anything about the driver, but I recently thought about how different my childhood would have been had my family spent years in courts, bitterly pursuing justice. Instead, I grew up inspired by my brother's memory. Yes, we grieved terribly. But my sister-in-law's choice shows me that forgiveness can save the life of a child. I hope to save my kids too.

FAMILY PRAYER *(Hold hands together as you pray.)*

Parent: Our Father, who art in heaven, hallowed be your name...

All: Your kingdom come, your will be done on earth as it is in heaven...

Parent Give us this day our daily bread...

All: And forgive us our trespasses, as we forgive those who trespass against us...

Parent: And lead us not into temptation, but deliver us from evil.

Invite your family to say "Amen" a few times—in big voices and small, quiet voices.

FAMILY ACTIVITY

Have your family create Easter wish lists of spiritual things they want for themselves and the world. They might include greater patience, more time together in prayer, world peace, or forgiveness. Display your lists and pray about them.

JONAH 3:1–10 » LUKE 11:29–32

WHALE TALES

"This generation is an evil generation; it seeks a sign,
but no sign will be given it, except the sign of Jonah." LUKE 11:29

I always thought Jonah built a fire in the belly of the whale, saved his dad, and then became a real boy. Wait. I may have gotten Jonah confused with another story. Our childhood perceptions can stay with us, which is why learning about our faith isn't just for our kids. The story of Jonah merits reading with adult eyes to catch all the delicious ironies and the beauty of God's mercy. Briefly, God commands Jonah to tell the people of Nineveh to repent of their evil ways. Jonah feels weak and unqualified. He tries to flee, wreaking havoc along the way. God pursues Jonah and shows him that he really can complete his mission. Sound like anyone you know?

FAMILY PRAYER

Parent: Forty days, forty days. Lead us, Lord, in all your ways.
  All: Forty days, forty days. We get ready in many ways.
Parent: Moses walked for forty years, Jesus fasted forty days.
  All: Forty days, forty days. We get ready in many ways.
Parent: Lead us, Lord, in all your ways, with fasting, alms, and prayers
    of praise.
  All: Forty days, forty days. We get ready in many ways. Amen!

Have your kids act out Moses walking and Jesus fasting as you pray.

FAMILY ACTIVITY

Today's a great day to catch some classic biblical movies with your kids. Try *Jonah: a VeggieTales Movie*, or DreamWorks's *The Prince of Egypt*.

ESTHER C:12, 14–16, 23–25 » MATTHEW 7:7–12

ACTION HERO

"Ask and it will be given to you; seek and you will find;
knock and the door will be opened to you." MATTHEW 7:7

I break into a cold sweat whenever I recall the door-to-door fundraising of childhood. Trembling, I'd carry my box of chocolates up neighbors' walkways, ring doorbells, and pray no one was home. So even now the idea of knocking at the door unsettles me. But Jesus doesn't want us passively waiting for answers to prayer. He wants us to ask, seek, and knock—to take action. That might mean working on needless worry and trusting in God. It might mean removing yourself from an unhealthful work situation or helping a child in moral trouble. Yes, it's scary. But Jesus isn't on the other side of the door. He's standing next to us. I wish I'd learned that long ago.

FAMILY PRAYER *(Kids can act out asking, seeking, and knocking.)*
Parent: Lord God, sometimes we forget to pray.
   All: We ask. We seek. We knock.
Parent: Sometimes we want you to give us exactly what we want.
   All: We ask. We seek. We knock.
Parent: Help us, Lord, to pray that your will be done.
   All: We ask. We seek. We knock. Amen.

Ask all to share the name of someone they will pray for today.

FAMILY ACTIVITY
It's over a week since Lent began. Today, review your family Lent commitments. If anyone has messed up, that's okay. Just start again.

EZEKIEL 18:21–28 » MATTHEW 5:20–26

WORDS WITH FAMILIES

You say, "The LORD's way is not fair!"...Is it my way that is unfair, or rather, are not your ways unfair? EZEKIEL 18:25

My friend Nancy tells of a time her two teenagers made a certain offensive word part of their regular vocabulary. Nancy tried everything, but the word continued. So when her sons invited a group of friends over, Nancy engaged them all in conversation, freely and loudly punctuating her sentences with that word. Her sons stared in wide-eyed shock and embarrassment. But they never used the word in her presence again. Our kids might not understand us sometimes. They might say our parenting ways are unfair, but we see another view. We can take comfort in the fact that God sees this view too. He's got our backs.

FAMILY PRAYER

Parent: Lord God, sometimes we wonder why things
are the way they are.
All: God loves me forever and ever.
Parent: We ask why bad things happen sometimes.
All: God loves me forever and ever.
Parent: But we remember, Lord, that you love us.
You stay with us through good and bad.
All: God loves me forever and ever. Amen.

If a disaster or other difficult event has happened recently, talk and pray about it.

FAMILY ACTIVITY

Find a way to help the helpers. You might bake treats for your fire or police department, or bring a flower to your school crossing guard.

DEUTERONOMY 26:16–19 » MATTHEW 5:43–48

ROOT RULES

The LORD, your God, commands you to observe these statutes and decrees. Be careful, then, to observe them with all your heart and with all your soul. DEUTERONOMY 26:16

It surprised me to learn that the word "rule" comes from the Latin *regula*, which is the root for "regular." The Rule of St. Benedict wasn't so much about rules as it was a way for Benedictine monks to live in a regular rhythm of prayer, work, reflection, and rest leading to God. I like to think of the church's rules in the same way. They're made to help God's children get to his kingdom safely. We may not always understand their face value, but it doesn't mean we reject rules outright. Instead, we learn what's behind them. It usually comes down to a single root: love.

FAMILY PRAYER

Parent: Father, sometimes it feels like winter will never end.

All: Spring, summer, fall, winter. We love you always.

Parent: But you have a plan for everything.

All: Spring, summer, fall, winter. We love you always.

Parent: Our spring will come, as it always does. Help us wait patiently.

All: Spring, summer, fall, winter. We love you always. Amen.

Invite everyone to share a favorite winter memory.

FAMILY ACTIVITY

The Easter date depends on seasonal rhythms. It's always the first Sunday after the first full moon after the equinox (March 21). Start a family practice of observing the moon and its changes each night during Lent.

Genesis 15:5–12, 17–18 » Philippians 3:17—4:1 » Luke 9:28b–36

TOWER OF BABBLING

But he did not know what he was saying. Luke 9:33

Jesus has just appeared in his heavenly glory, and nothing like this has ever happened to Peter. So our poor fisherman hero babbles about tents. I get that. The moment I saw my first baby in all his glory, I'm sure I babbled about Lord knows what, and worried about my share of tents. How would I care for this tiny, wondrous being? How would I feed him, love him, and not make him completely insecure by age five? God can break through the clutter when our thoughts run crazy. We just have to let him in. How? Next time your thoughts overpower you, make the sign of the cross. It's the surest way to peace.

FAMILY PRAYER

Parent: In the name of the Father and of the Son
and of the Holy Spirit.
All: We belong to you, God.
Parent: Father, Son, and Holy Spirit, guide our thoughts.
All: We belong to you, God.
Parent: Guide our words and actions all the days of our lives.
All: We belong to you, God. Amen.

*With your thumb, trace a small cross on everyone's forehead
as a sign you all belong to God.*

FAMILY ACTIVITY

Before Mass today, talk to your children about observing the cross in church. Ask them to silently look for the cross and the ways we show reverence for it. Afterward, talk about their observations.

1 Peter 5:1–4 » Matthew 16:13–19

HEAVEN ON EARTH

Jesus said to him in reply, "Blessed are you, Simon son of Jonah.
For flesh and blood has not revealed this to you,
but my heavenly Father." Matthew 16:17

Some of the high school kids in our parish drive themselves to church on Sunday while their parents stay home. A lot of parents find it necessary to explain their reasons. "My kid goes for me...I'm exhausted on Sunday and God understands...I don't get anything out of it." Maybe it's true that some homilies are dull, and that we're too overworked to spend an hour in a pew. But the Mass is where heaven is revealed. It's where we receive Jesus in the Eucharist. Not a symbol or gesture of Jesus, but the real Jesus—body, blood, soul, and divinity. Who could miss that?

FAMILY PRAYER
Parent: Father in heaven, bless those who lead us in faith.
  All: They are signs of your love.
Parent: Help them complete the work you've begun.
  All: They are signs of your love.
Parent: Help us help them proclaim your love to the whole world.
  All: They are signs of your love. Amen.

Pray in silence for clergy, religious, and all who lead us in faith.

FAMILY ACTIVITY
Today is the Feast of the Chair of St. Peter. Pray as a family for our Holy Father today. Get his words of wisdom at his Twitter feed: twitter.com/pontifex.

ISAIAH 1:10, 16–20 » MATTHEW 23:1–12

GREAT SERVICE

"The greatest among you must be your servant." MATTHEW 23:11

Many adults give up on the church because of what they hear in today's gospel. They see clergy and lay leaders "tying heavy burdens" on others' shoulders. They see hypocrisy and faults. So like pioneers or entrepreneurs, they strike out on their own, following Jesus their way. But is that what Jesus wants when he says, "The greatest among you must be your servant"? If we're really following Jesus, we'll recognize we're all sinners and servants. Jesus didn't turn his back on sinners. He ate with them. He washed their feet. He gave up his life for hypocrites and sinners. How can I serve my fellow sinners today?

FAMILY PRAYER

Parent: Lord Jesus, you lived, suffered, died, and rose from the dead.
   All: The Lord our God is one.
Parent: You didn't choose who you'd save and who you wouldn't.
   All: The Lord our God is one.
Parent: You give all of us life and love. We thank you as one family,
      one church.
   All: The Lord our God is one. Amen.

Invite all to think of those who might need your help today.

FAMILY ACTIVITY

Does your parish take part in Operation Rice Bowl? Keep the cardboard container at your dinner table and find a way for your family to make some small sacrifices so that your donation comes from the heart.

JEREMIAH 18:18–20 » MATTHEW 20:17–28

GOAL TENDING

"Command that these two sons of mine sit, one at your right and the other at your left, in your kingdom." MATTHEW 20:21

Can you blame the mother of James and John? She only wants what's best for her kids. But if she knew the path Jesus saw for her boys—suffering and martyrdom—would she still have been so bold? Lent is a good time to think about our goals for our kids. College? Career success? Happiness? When it comes down to it, is there any goal better than their happiness in heaven (and yours, too)? Can you see the path that leads there? What changes might you make during this lenten season to help you correct your family's course? A prayer or two can help.

FAMILY PRAYER *(Response, Psalm 31)*
Parent: Lord Jesus, sometimes it's hard to follow you.
　　All: Our trust is in the Lord.
Parent: Your path is the way of the cross. Help us walk with you.
　　All: Our trust is in the Lord.
Parent: Lord Jesus, you don't just lead us. You carry us
　　　　 when things get tough.
　　All: Our trust is in the Lord. Amen.

Invite everyone to close their eyes and imagine Jesus at their side.

FAMILY ACTIVITY
Trace your kids' feet onto construction paper and help your children trim them. Let them write or draw their lenten promises on the cutouts and display them wherever you keep your family's shoes.

JEREMIAH 17:5–10 » LUKE 16:19–31

POWER LINES

I, the LORD, alone probe the mind and test the heart. JEREMIAH 17:10

The online prayer request was hard to ignore. A mom wrote about a family member whose terrible decisions were leading him to possible jail time. I didn't know this mom personally, but I felt her anguish. A week or so later she e-mailed to report an astonishing turn of events. This family member had thanked her for the prayers and told her that God had revealed himself to him. He tearfully confided that he could now see this chain of events as "necessary for his salvation." And he who had always mocked prayer was now saying the Rosary daily. Who needs your prayers today?

FAMILY PRAYER
(Meditate on a Rosary mystery [see below] as you say one decade.)

On the large bead say an Our Father:
Parent: Our Father who art in heaven…
   All: Give us this day our daily bread…

On each small bead say a Hail Mary:
Parent: Hail Mary, full of grace, the Lord is with thee…
   All: Holy Mary, mother of God, pray for us sinners…

Invite family members to mention someone they'd like to pray for.

FAMILY ACTIVITY
To help kids meditate on a Rosary mystery, invite them to use their senses to imagine it. They might color a picture of the angel visiting Mary, create the scene with Legos, or act it out. To learn about the Rosary mysteries, visit www.familyrosary.org.

GENESIS 37:3–4, 12–13A, 17B–28A » MATTHEW 21:33–43, 45–46

FAMILY TIES

Come on, let us kill him and throw him into one of the cisterns here; we could say that a wild beast devoured him. GENESIS 37:20

Joseph and his brothers are the ultimate dysfunctional family. His brothers consider killing Joseph but decide to throw him in a cistern and then sell him as a slave for twenty pieces of silver. Can you imagine the long-term effects on poor Joseph? I'm thinking he'd need some pretty serious therapy. But (spoiler alert), Joseph meets the brothers again in the Book of Genesis. And after playing a little prank on them (I'd say they deserved more), he forgives them. We think of Old Testament justice as an eye for an eye, but Joseph surprises us. He shows that nobody is above forgiving, even real brothers and sisters.

FAMILY PRAYER

Parent: Lord God, watch over our family and guide us always.
    All: Our Father, our family.
Parent: Keep us safe and true to you.
    All: Our Father, our family.
Parent: Help us love each other, listen to each other, and forgive each other always.
    All: Our Father, our family. Amen.

Have a family "group hug."

FAMILY ACTIVITY

Write the letters of the word "forgive" on seven small sheets of paper and have family members work together to form words from them. How many new words can you create together?

MICAH 7:14–15, 18–20 » LUKE 15:1–3, 11–32

ROCK YOUR WORLD

You will cast into the depths of the sea all our sins;
you will show faithfulness to Jacob, and grace to Abraham,
as you have sworn to our fathers from days of old.

MICAH 7:19–20

In Old Testament times, a jubilee was a yearlong period that occurred every fifty years, and it was a big deal. Slaves were freed, debts were forgiven, and lands that had been taken or confiscated were returned to their original owners. Imagine how much the jubilee rocked people's worlds! Pope Francis has named 2016 a jubilee year to celebrate the joy of mercy. He's not looking for symbols or gestures. He wants us to rock the world. What will you and your family do to be merciful? And how will you celebrate God's mercy in your life? Read all of today's gospel and think about it.

FAMILY PRAYER *(Response: Psalm 103)*
Parent: Lord God, you give us so much.
   All: The Lord is kind and merciful.
Parent: Help us appreciate what we have, instead of looking for more.
   All: The Lord is kind and merciful.
Parent: Help us use your gifts well, every day and in every way.
   All: The Lord is kind and merciful. Amen.

Ask everyone to mention a gift they've received from God.

FAMILY ACTIVITY
Write down the gifts from God your family mentioned in their prayer. Now ask everyone to think about how they'd feel if they didn't have those gifts. Brainstorm ways you might use your gifts to help those who go without.

EXODUS 3:1–8A, 13–15 » 1 CORINTHIANS 10:1–6, 10–12 » LUKE 13:1–9
or (YEAR A) EXODUS 17:3–7 » ROMANS 5:1–2, 5–8 » JOHN 4:5–42

COMMUNITY GARDENING

"Sir, leave it for this year also, and I shall cultivate the ground around it and fertilize it; it may bear fruit in the future." LUKE 13:8

Over coffee one evening, some moms and I shared the challenges our sons faced at the moment. I said I'd pray, but knew I'd forget, so I sent myself an e-mail reminder once a week, copying my friends. Word spread and now, three years later, more than eighty moms pray for hundreds of sons and grandsons every Friday morning, wherever we are—work, home, school, or vacation. One mom started a group for daughters too. Our little community works patiently, cultivating a rich soil of prayer. Just reading that list of names affects us deeply. Best of all, we know our prayers bear fruit in ways we can see and in ways we can't.

FAMILY PRAYER
Parent: Father, you know and love each person in our great big world.
    All: Bless the Lord, O my soul.
Parent: How is it possible to know each of us so deeply?
    All: Bless the Lord, O my soul.
Parent: But for you, Lord, nothing is impossible.
    All: Bless the Lord, O my soul. Amen.

Pray silently for all who have no one to pray for them.

FAMILY ACTIVITY
During Lent, many people prepare to be fully received into the Catholic Church. Show your children the photos of your parish's catechumens and candidates (on the website or in back of church), and add these folks to your family prayers.

2 Kings 5:1–15b » Luke 4:24–30

TOUGH TEACHER

They rose up, drove him out of the town, and led him to the brow of the hill...to hurl him down headlong. Luke 4:29

Jesus has just finished telling his fellow citizens that no prophet is accepted in his own town, and they try to drive him out—of his own hometown. You wonder if later that night anyone in Nazareth sat up in bed and said, "Hey, wait a second. Didn't we do exactly what Jesus said people do to prophets? Wouldn't that make Jesus...a prophet?" Jesus always speaks the truth. The question is, do we share all of his teachings with our families, or do we drive out the tough things we don't want to hear? This is a tough one. Help us on this, Jesus.

FAMILY PRAYER
Parent: Father, thank you for communities: our family, school, parish, and city.
All: Bless your people, Lord.
Parent: Help us understand others and live in peace.
All: Bless your people, Lord.
Parent: Help us share your love with all.
All: Bless your people, Lord. Amen.

Pray silently for peace.

FAMILY ACTIVITY
Stand face to face with your kids as you wiggle your fingers slightly. Let your kids imitate you with a slightly bigger wiggle—maybe with their hands. Keep going back and forth making the action larger until everyone wiggles their entire bodies. Talk about how peace starts with small acts.

DANIEL 3:25, 34–43 » MATTHEW 18:21–35

FACE OF FORGIVENESS

*"Lord, if my brother sins against me, how often must I forgive him?
As many as seven times?"* MATTHEW 18:21

Peter can't possibly know that he himself will need forgiveness over and over. Pope Francis tells us to think about Jesus' response when Peter finally understands the magnitude of his three-time denial of Jesus. "He meets the gaze of Jesus who patiently, wordlessly, says to him, 'Peter, don't be afraid of your weakness; trust in me.'" Pope Francis tells us how beautiful and tender Jesus' gaze is. How does forgiveness look in your home? Is it practiced with tenderness and patience, over and over again? This is something I need to work on at my house.

FAMILY PRAYER *(Response based on Psalm 25:6)*
Parent: Lord God, you are so patient with us.
    All: Remember your mercy, O Lord.
Parent: When we sin, you forgive us over and over again.
    All: Remember your mercy, O Lord.
Parent: All you ask is that we do the same for others. Help us forgive, Lord. It's not always easy.
    All: Remember your mercy, O Lord. Amen.

Invite everyone to think of someone who might need forgiveness right now.

FAMILY ACTIVITY
Pope Francis calls on all Catholics to take part in "24 Hours for the Lord," beginning this Friday afternoon. Today, find out where and how you can receive the sacrament of reconciliation at your parish. Then commit to taking your family to the sacrament this weekend.

DEUTERONOMY 4:1, 5–9 » MATTHEW 5:17–19

MIRROR, MIRROR

"Therefore, whoever breaks one of the least of these commandments and teaches others to do so will be called least in the kingdom of heaven." MATTHEW 5:19

I once heard about a chapel with nothing in it but a chair and a mirror. Penitents go there to prepare for confession. It sounds incredibly tough, but really, that's what Lent is. We strip away everything and look honestly in the mirror. When we're able to see our faults, weaknesses, and sins, we take them to God for help and forgiveness. Then we start fresh. A daily examination of conscience is a good habit to have. It's not about beating yourself up, but seeing where you can improve.

FAMILY PRAYER *(An examination of conscience)*
Parent: Today, Lord, we ask ourselves how we can get closer to you.
    All: Jesus, help me do better.
Parent: I ask, am I patient and kind? Do I say "thank you"?
        Do I tell the truth?
    All: Jesus, help me do better.
Parent: Do I listen at Mass? Do I listen to others? Do I forgive?
        Do I play fair?
    All: Jesus, help me do better.
Parent: Jesus, help us look honestly at ourselves. Just trying
        to get better brings us closer to you.

Say an act of contrition together.

FAMILY ACTIVITY
Get everyone ready for reconciliation with an examination of conscience (above). Don't answer the questions aloud. Just give everyone time to think about them.

Jeremiah 7:23–28 » Luke 11:14–23

HEALTHY FAMILIES

*Faithfulness has disappeared; the word itself
is banished from their speech.* Jeremiah 7:28

If you were to talk to a random group of parents about your child's purity, chances are they'd think you were eliminating processed food or refined sugars. A lot of good words like purity, holiness, and faithfulness have been banished from our vocabulary these days. The world tries to convince us that these are values from another era and keep modern families from achieving our goals. But staying faithful to Christ is freeing, not confining. When families live the Beatitudes or keep the Corporal Works of Mercy, we rise above the world's narrow viewpoint. We see beyond the trends and live God's incredible plan for us. Now that's healthy living.

FAMILY PRAYER
Parent: Lord God, we ask you to keep our family holy
　　　　and healthy.
　All: You are our God, and we are your people.
Parent: Lord God, we ask you to keep us pure.
　All: You are our God, and we are your people.
Parent: Lord God, we ask you to keep us faithful to you in all things.
　All: You are our God, and we are your people. Amen.

Pray silently for everyone in our church family.

FAMILY ACTIVITY
Have a conversation with your family about confession. If it's been a while, review the steps. You can find a great video at outsidedabox. com. Click on the "Films" tab, then search "confession."

HOSEA 14:2–10 » MARK 12:28–34

PATHS TO GLORY

Straight are the paths of the LORD, in them the just walk...

HOSEA 14:10

First Friday devotion is an old Catholic tradition based on a promise our Lord made to St. Margaret Mary Alacoque—that those who receive Holy Communion on nine consecutive First Fridays will receive the grace of final repentance. "My Heart will be their secure refuge in that last hour." My mom made heroic efforts to get to First Friday Mass, but something always seemed to happen on the eighth or ninth Friday—a sick child or some other emergency. God doesn't have a Mass attendance sheet; he's pleased any time we travel a path to him.

FAMILY PRAYER *(Based on the Jewish daily prayer, the Shema)*
Parent: Hear, Israel, the Lord is our God. The Lord is One.
  All: Blessed be his name forever and ever.
Parent: We will love the Lord our God with all our hearts, with all our souls, with all our minds, and with all our strength.
  All: Blessed be his name forever and ever.
Parent: And we shall love our neighbors as ourselves. Amen.

Repeat the prayer slowly, inviting all to think of the blessings they have received.

FAMILY ACTIVITY
You've made plans to take your family to confession. After the sacrament, make sure to include a fun celebration of God's forgiveness. Maybe go to a movie together or get ice cream.

HOSEA 6:1–6 » LUKE 18:9–14

PACKING MY SINS

But the tax collector stood off at a distance and would not even raise his eyes to heaven but beat his breast and prayed, "O God, be merciful to me a sinner." LUKE 18:13

St. Josephine Bakhita said that when she died she would bring two suitcases. One would carry her sins and the other, much heavier, would hold the merits of Jesus. Hiding the ugly suitcase behind Jesus' merits she would ask God's judgment based on what was before him. "Oh," the good saint said, "I'm sure I won't be sent away!" It's true that before God, we are all sinners, even the holiest among us. Nothing but God's overflowing mercy can save us. That gives us hope that our family can someday join Josephine, who added, "I'll turn toward St. Peter and I'll say, 'Close the door because I'm staying here.'"

FAMILY PRAYER
Place the Stations of the Cross (see below) around your home and walk among them slowly. Place yourselves there with Jesus as you pray at each station:

Parent: We adore you, O Christ, and we bless you,
   All: Because by your holy cross, you have redeemed
      the world.

Invite your children to return to any station that has meaning for them right now and spend time in prayer there.

FAMILY ACTIVITY
Plan a visit to your church and look at the Stations of the Cross together. Or search for Stations of the Cross coloring pages on the Internet.

JOSHUA 5:9A, 10–12 » 2 CORINTHIANS 5:17–21 » LUKE 15:1–3, 11–32
OR (YEAR A) 1 SAMUEL 16:1B, 6–7, 10–13A » EPHESIANS 5:8–14 » JOHN 9:1–41

LIFE ON THE EDGE

*"Then let us celebrate with a feast, because this son of mine
was dead, and has come to life again."* LUKE 15:23–24

Imagine your kids never going outside, ever. No snowball fights, soccer playing, puddle jumping, or tree climbing. Frightening thought, isn't it? Yet in a way, we keep ourselves confined all the time. Pope Francis says that when we stay inside our comfort zones, life can get depressing and unhealthful. But, he says, Jesus wants us to travel to the outskirts, and encounter life. Yes, it's risky. But so is swimming in a lake, and we'd never deny our children that kind of adventure. At the beginning of Lent, your family committed to helping a particular group. Is there something you know you still have to do for them? Pray about it today, and then go do it.

FAMILY PRAYER

Parent: This is the day the Lord has made.
   All: Let us rejoice and be glad.
Parent: Today, God, we remember that you love us so much
         you've given us your only Son.
   All: Let us rejoice and be glad.
Parent: Everyone who believes in him will have eternal life.
   All: Let us rejoice and be glad.

Rejoice with hugs all around!

FAMILY ACTIVITY

Today is World Day of Prayer and Laetare Sunday, Lent's halfway point. Why not have a family feast to celebrate? Let everyone help with cooking, decorations, and table setting or cleanup.

ISAIAH 65:17–21 » JOHN 4:43–54

MILES TO WALK

*The father realized that just at that time Jesus had said to him,
"Your son will live," and he and his whole household came to believe.*

JOHN 4:53

I know so many parents who struggle with their teens or adult children who don't believe or receive the sacraments. These good parents blame themselves bitterly and search for things they might have done differently. So it's good to think of the dad in today's gospel. He can't text his wife and check his son's progress. He simply has to trust in Jesus' words: "Your son will live." Now the dad has to walk away, believing. Look at the added benefit of his patient faith—his whole household comes to believe. Sometimes we have to keep walking and trusting, even when we can't see what's ahead for our kids.

FAMILY PRAYER

Parent: Lord, we like to think we can do things on our own.
But you're always with us, guiding us, helping us.

All: Jesus, I trust in you.

Parent: With you, O God, we can do anything.
Help us remember that.

All: Jesus, I trust in you. Amen.

Invite everyone to pray silently for strength to accomplish their goals.

FAMILY ACTIVITY

Is your family room floor littered with toys? Use the mess to play a trust-building game. One person is blindfolded while another guides them through the "minefield." Don't forget to blindfold yourself and let your kids guide you, too!

EZEKIEL 47:1–9, 12 » JOHN 5:1–16

DUSTING ADVICE

Along both banks of the river, fruit trees of every kind shall grow; their leaves shall not fade, nor their fruit fail...for they shall be watered by the flow from the sanctuary. EZEKIEL 47:12

A sign in the planter reads, "Please don't water, even if we seem to need it." Apparently some well-meaning parishioners hadn't noticed the drip irrigation system in the potted petunias outside our church doors when they took it upon themselves to do some watering. The plants drowned and died. As people of the sanctuary, we are caretakers of God's creation, but we need signs and warnings. Who better to guide us than our shepherd, Pope Francis? In his encyclical *Laudato Si', On Care for Our Common Home,* he reminds us of our connectedness: "We have forgotten that we ourselves are dust of the earth; our very bodies are made up of her elements, we breathe her air and we receive life and refreshment from her waters." The lenten spring is a good time to remember this.

FAMILY PRAYER

All: Praise be to you, my Lord, for creating...

Invite everyone to finish the sentence.

FAMILY ACTIVITY

Take prayerful Catholic action with your family by learning about issues of justice and human dignity. Some great places to begin are togoforth.org (a blog of the USCCB inspired by Pope Francis) and catholicclimatecovenant.org.

Isaiah 49:8–15 » John 5:17–30

MOTHERS' CLUB

*Can a mother forget her infant, be without tenderness
for the child of her womb?* Isaiah 49:15

A friend of mine, raised in a Protestant tradition, pointed at a Mary statue in my kitchen. "I totally get why Catholics love Mary," she said. That wasn't something I expected to hear, and my jaw dropped nearly to the floor. But maybe I shouldn't have been surprised. My friend has endured some painful losses: the death of her father, followed by the death of her best friend. Then a diagnosis of cancer for my friend herself. I'm sure she has spent many days and nights in the spiritual arms of our Blessed Mother. Mary doesn't categorize us as Catholic, Protestant, Jewish, Muslim, or Hindu. She's a mom who sees only children to love.

FAMILY PRAYER *(This prayer, written in about 300 AD, is the oldest known prayer to the mother of Jesus.)*
Parent and All: We turn to you for protection, Holy Mother of God. Listen to our prayers and help us in our needs. Save us from every danger, glorious and blessed Virgin.

Invite everyone to repeat the prayer, mentioning any needs or special intentions.

FAMILY ACTIVITY
From the oldest prayer to the newest: compose your own family prayer to Mary. Display it in your home.

EXODUS 32:7–14 » JOHN 5:31–47

COMFORT ZONE

"How can you believe, when you accept praise from one another and do not seek the praise that comes from the only God?" JOHN 5:44

She comes home in tears, and you learn that a group of kindergarten classmates refused to play with her. Rejection. It can start early and hurt deeply. A hug, a pep talk, and maybe an extra twenty minutes of story time tonight might help, but as she gets older, it will get more challenging. That's when parents can feel helpless and frustrated. But the light of hope is that God loves our children unconditionally. When we start that conversation early, repeat it at every opportunity, and back it up by showing the same love, our kids will be okay. Really.

FAMILY PRAYER

Parent: Lord God, thank you for inviting us to your house. We know you welcome us with love and joy. You don't expect gifts, flowers, or anything else. Yet you give us everything. The moment we enter your house, we know you are here, even if we can't see you. And because your love is endless, we know you are with us when we leave your holy presence. Thank you, Lord.

All: Amen.

Say this prayer (or something like it) before going to Mass or visiting your church.

FAMILY ACTIVITY

Plan a church visit. Let your children touch the statues and dip their fingers in the baptismal font. Explain that Jesus is present in the tabernacle, and let them get up close and personal.

31

WISDOM 2:1A, 12–22 » JOHN 7:1–2, 10, 25–30

BURIED IN DOUBT

The wicked said among themselves, thinking not aright: "Let us beset the just one, because he is obnoxious to us." WISDOM 2:12

A friend tells me that doubts beset her. So she gave up trying to believe in God. I tell her I struggle with my faith too, and that even saints like Joan of Arc struggled. My friend (who is a scientist) says that's irrelevant. I ask if scientists walk away from conclusions that are hard to accept. She says that until I have proof of God's existence, we can't discuss it, and walks away. I'm left alone, thinking I could have handled this better. I could have asked sincere questions, rather than snarky ones. I pray for my friend. I pray for her children and for my children. I pray that God will strengthen both of us in our weakness and give us the grace we need.

FAMILY PRAYER

Parent: Lord God, thank you for the good food you provide.
  All: Bless us, O Lord.
Parent: Jesus, make us strong in your love and goodness.
  All: Bless us, O Lord.
Parent: Holy Spirit, send down your grace on our family.
  All: Bless us, O Lord. Amen.

Ask everyone to name something they love about another family member.

FAMILY ACTIVITY

Who says meatless Fridays have to be joyless? Have an indoor picnic, serve dinner by candlelight, or pretend the dinner table is a boat and you're the apostles "fishing" for tuna sandwiches.

Jeremiah 11:18–20 » John 7:40–53

GET SMARTER

"Does our law condemn a man before it first hears him and finds out what he is doing?" John 7:51

My seven-year-old had been playing all morning, so when I said it was time to get ready for Mass and he replied that his stomach hurt, I was naturally suspicious. He hadn't said anything all morning. But he stuck with his story and I stubbornly stuck by my conviction that he wasn't sick. He moaned on the way to church and held his stomach, but I didn't buy it. Sitting in the pew he asked if he could go to the bathroom. I walked him to the parish hall, lecturing all the way. And as I waited outside the restroom, I heard the distinctive sound of my son getting sick. Lesson learned? I'm not as smart as I think I am. I need to listen to my children before I make judgments.

FAMILY PRAYER

Parent: Lord God, you gave us eyes to see your goodness.

   All: I hear; I listen; I respond.

Parent: You gave us ears to hear your truth.

   All: I hear; I listen; I respond.

Parent: Help us listen well and see clearly, especially when others
   need us.

   All: I hear; I listen; I respond. Amen.

Invite all to share something they saw or heard today that reminded them of God's goodness.

FAMILY ACTIVITY

Do your kids know any worship songs? Go to www.spiritandsong.com to download songs (you can find some for free) and learn about Catholic recording artists. You can even find a lenten playlist.

Isaiah 43:16–21 » Philippians 3:8–14 » John 8:1–11
or (Year A) Ezekiel 37:12–14 » Romans 8:8–11 » John 11:1–45

THANKING HEAVEN

*Jesus said to her, "Did I not tell you that if you believe
you will see the glory of God?"* John 11:40

I ran into a friend at church the other day. She'd just run a half marathon, but she didn't look exhausted (the way I'd look if I'd managed even a quarter, or an eighth, of a marathon). But there's much more to her story. My friend's husband left years ago and she'd been raising their teenage son alone. She'd fought cancer so recently that she still wore a baseball cap to cover up the ravages of chemotherapy. Her family lives in Africa, so her support group here is small. Yet here she was at Mass. She wasn't asking for an end to her suffering, but thanking God for today. This is the kind of faith I pray for.

FAMILY PRAYER

Parent: Lord God, we join your whole church in praying
for those who need help.
All: Lord, hear our prayer.
Parent: We pray for all those who don't know you.
All: Lord, hear our prayer.
Parent: We pray for all those who are sick.
All: Lord, hear our prayer.

Add your own intentions and respond with "Lord, hear our prayer."

FAMILY ACTIVITY

On the way to and from Mass today, talk to your kids about the Prayer of the Faithful (the prayer petitions we make after we say the Creed). After Mass, ask if any prayers moved them particularly. At dinner, pray for these intentions again.

DANIEL 13:1–9, 15–17, 19–30, 33–62 *OR* 13:41C–62 » JOHN 8:1–11 *OR* JOHN 8:12–20

MYSTERY IN THE SAND

*Jesus bent down and began to write
on the ground with his finger.* JOHN 8:6

The gospel writer never reveals what Jesus writes here. Some theologians say Jesus writes to show his authority as author of the new law, since the law of Moses was written with "the finger of God." Others say Jesus writes the names of the woman's partners, or about forgiveness. It will probably always be a mystery. For many people, forgiveness itself is a mystery. How can God forgive heinous crimes and sins against humanity? Surely some criminals don't deserve God's forgiveness, do they? But could you refuse to forgive your own child? Would you say you'd forgive one but not the other? Our Father's mercy is boundless, mysterious, and not completely understood by mere humans. Read today's gospel again and contemplate this great mystery.

FAMILY PRAYER *(The Jesus Prayer)*
Parent: O Lord Jesus Christ, Son of God, have mercy on me, a sinner.
   All: O Lord Jesus Christ, Son of God, have mercy on me, a sinner.

Pray in silence, asking God to forgive your sins.

FAMILY ACTIVITY
The Jesus Prayer, above, is such a simple but powerful prayer. It's easy to memorize, making it something kids can remember and reach for any time. Some people recommend saying it as a preparation for receiving Holy Communion. Teach it to your children today.

Numbers 21:4–9 » John 8:21–30

REFRESH AND RECHARGE

But with their patience worn out by the journey, the people complained against God and Moses, "Why have you brought us up from Egypt to die in this desert?" Numbers 21:4–5

You might feel a little like Moses' followers right now. Let's face it, the lenten journey is long. Spring seems far away. And how many cheese-pizza Fridays can you deal with? St. Josemaría Escrivá once said, "To begin is for everyone. To persevere is for saints." Now before you go thinking you're not a saint, consider this: What big challenges have you overcome in life? You're already a saint for persevering there. Lent is small potatoes. If you still need a refresher today, look for someone who needs your family's help. (You won't have to look far.) That's a sure way to turn your day around.

FAMILY PRAYER

Parent: Lord, we pray for all who have died—those we know and those we haven't met.

All: Let your light shine on them, Lord.

Parent: May they rest forever in your joy.

All: Let your light shine on them, Lord.

Parent: Bless their families, Lord, and all who are sad. Help them know you are with them.

All: Let your light shine on them, Lord. Amen.

(Pray silently together.)

FAMILY ACTIVITY

Make a family shrine to honor the dead. (Yes, pets count too.) Include photos and drawings—anything that comforts and helps your family pray.

DANIEL 3:14–20, 91–92, 95 » JOHN 8:31–42

GREAT SAVE

"If you remain in my word, you will truly be my disciples, and you will know the truth, and the truth will set you free." JOHN 8:31–32

You've probably heard the airline safety announcement that goes something like this: If you are travelling with a child, secure your oxygen mask first, before assisting your child. You know where I'm going with this, right? Yes, we adults can be weak. We sometimes question our faith. We can get bored at Mass and annoyed with our fellow Christians. But we owe it to our children to accept our own weaknesses and keep working on them. We can't save our kids if we don't breathe freely. Today, grab your oxygen mask—a rosary, a Bible, a crucifix, or whatever you need to find Jesus' truth. Meditate on it. Take as long as you need. The truth really will save you and set you free.

FAMILY PRAYER

Parent: Blessed are the poor in spirit, those who rely on God.
   All: Jesus, your truth sets us free.
Parent: Blessed are the meek and humble.
   All: Jesus, your truth sets us free.
Parent: Blessed are the clean of heart.
   All: Jesus, your truth sets us free.

"Blessed are…" Invite family members to finish the sentence.

FAMILY ACTIVITY

Today, pick a chapter of your child's religion book, one of today's Mass readings, or a saint story. What light can you gain from it that you might shine for your child?

FAMILY SAINTS

"Amen, amen, I say to you, whoever keeps my word will never see death." JOHN 8:51

My father-in-law wasn't a church-going man. But he was a man of quiet faith, and he beat death once during World War II when, as a young Marine stationed in the Pacific, he contracted rheumatic fever. Paul was a member of The Greatest Generation, so dubbed by newsman Tom Brokaw in his book of the same title. Like others of his time, my father-in-law grew up during the Great Depression and was familiar with hunger. He understood sacrifice and hard work, building seven houses with his own hands and sometimes working two jobs to support four children. Let's share the stories of our family saints with our kids. May we never forget their sacrifices.

FAMILY PRAYER *(Based on the Prayer of St. Patrick)*
Parent: Christ before me, Christ behind me, Christ within me.
   All: Christ, be with me.
Parent: Christ on my right, Christ on my left. Christ where I sleep, Christ where I sit, Christ where I rise.
   All: Christ, be with me.
Parent: Christ in every heart, every eye, and every ear. Christ be with us forever and ever.
   All: Christ, be with me. Amen.

In your own words, ask Jesus to be with your family today.

FAMILY ACTIVITY
According to tradition, St. Patrick used a shamrock to teach about the three Persons in the Holy Trinity. Today, use a picture or other object to share something about your ancestors with your kids.

JEREMIAH 20:10–13 » JOHN 10:31–42

CHAMPION OF MERCY

But the Lord is with me, like a mighty champion. Jeremiah 20:11

"This is the happiest day of my life," St. John Paul II declared. He'd just canonized Sister Faustina Kowalska and established the Feast of Divine Mercy. As he noted in his homily the first time the feast was celebrated, "Jesus said to Sr. Faustina one day: 'Mankind will not have peace until it turns with trust to my mercy.' Divine Mercy! This is the Easter gift that the Church receives from the risen Christ and offers to humanity at the dawn of the third millennium." St. John Paul II died on the eve of the Feast of the Divine Mercy in 2005. If this feast was so important to our beloved saint, maybe we need to take a closer look.

FAMILY PRAYER *(Chaplet of the Divine Mercy)*

Holding rosary beads in your hands, say this on the large bead:
Parent: Eternal Father, I offer you the Body and Blood, Soul and Divinity of your dearly beloved Son, our Lord Jesus Christ, in atonement for our sins and those of the whole world.

On each of the small beads say this:
Parent: For the sake of his sorrowful Passion,
All: Have mercy on us and on the whole world.

Continue saying the prayer on each of the beads.

FAMILY ACTIVITY
Begin saying the Chaplet of Divine Mercy every day between now and the Feast of Divine Mercy on April 3.

2 SAMUEL 7:4–5A, 12–14A, 16 » ROMANS 4:13, 16–18, 22
MATTHEW 1:16, 18–21, 24A OR LUKE 2:41–51A

PARENTING 101

He went down with them and came to Nazareth,
and was obedient to them. LUKE 2:51

He is one of the two most important people in Jesus' youth. Yet he never breathes a word in the gospels. In our collective imagination we see him: a quiet, mature, bearded man in brown robes, always carrying his trusty hammer or carpenter's square. But don't forget that Joseph is a man of principle and of action. He refuses to publicly humiliate Mary, even though it's within his rights. He gets moving when the angel tells him Jesus' life is in danger. Has Joseph ever even been to Egypt? Who knows? Does he speak the language? Probably not. But he doesn't worry about the obstacles, only what he has to do. That's the kind of parent I need to be.

FAMILY PRAYER

Parent: St. Joseph, you selflessly cared for Mary and Jesus.
   All: St. Joseph, pray for us.
Parent: Watch over our family too. Help all families in need.
   All: St. Joseph, pray for us.
Parent: Keep us safe when we travel, and always close
           to our loving Father.
   All: St. Joseph, pray for us.

Pray silently for all fathers and grandfathers.

FAMILY ACTIVITY

Make a lenten chore chart, with spring-cleaning jobs that can be done between now and Easter. For a reward, you might make St. Joseph cookies—sugar cookies in shapes symbolic of St. Joseph, like a staff, tools, or lilies.

LUKE 19:28–40 » ISAIAH 50:4–7 » PHILIPPIANS 2:6–11
LUKE 22:14—23:56 *OR* 23:1–49

YOUTH GROUP

Jesus proceeded on his journey up to Jerusalem. LUKE 19:28

Imagine two million kids flooding city streets, filling up parks, sleeping in tents, and going to Mass with the pope. That's World Youth Day. This summer, millions of young people from all over the world will converge on the city of Krakow, Poland, for this international event, which culminates in an enormous outdoor Mass celebrated by the Holy Father. Today, Palm Sunday, Pope Francis will bless all youth and young adults in St. Peter's Square. In like manner, during this coming Holy Week, we'll focus and pray each day for a particular group of young people. Let's start today by praying today for safe travels for the pope and all youth attending WYD this summer.

FAMILY PRAYER

Parent: Holy, holy, holy are you, God of hosts.

    All: Hosanna in the highest.

Parent: Heaven and earth are full of your glory.

    All: Hosanna in the highest.

Parent: Blessed is he who comes in the name of the Lord.

    All: Hosanna in the highest. Amen.

*Invite everyone to mention someone they will pray for
during Holy Week.*

FAMILY ACTIVITY

If you don't get palms at church, make some out of green construction paper. Or have kids dip their fingers in green finger paint and stamp a sheet of paper to create some mini palms.

ISAIAH 42:1–7 » JOHN 12:1–11

BIRTH-DAY

I, the LORD, have called you...I formed you... ISAIAH 42:6

Although the trees in your neighborhood may still be bare, they're full of new life. Back in the fall, when last year's leaves dropped, the new leaves were already there, inside teensy bud packages covered with tough, waterproof scales. Interestingly, scientists call these itty-bitty leaves that haven't yet appeared "leaves." They're not pre-leaves, or non-leaves. And they remain safe and protected until spring, when sap naturally rises from the tree's roots and spreads to the branches. The scales fall off the buds and those tiny, tender leaves appear, unfurling and growing. New life—who knew it had been there, through the very dead of winter? Today let's pray for protection for all unborn children.

FAMILY PRAYER

Parent: Lord God, today begins the holiest week of the year.
   All: Jesus, you are the light of the world.
Parent: Today begins the season of rebirth, too.
   All: Jesus, you are the light of the world.
Parent: Jesus, you bring hope when things seem hopeless,
       and light when things are darkest.
   All: Jesus, you are the light of the world. Amen.

Invite everyone to pray silently for people who need help this week.

FAMILY ACTIVITY

Celebrate spring by planning a resurrection garden, either indoors or outside. Measure off an area in the shape of a cross and choose flower or grass seed. Get the soil ready for planting this weekend.

ISAIAH 49:1–6 » JOHN 13:21–33, 36–38

HEAVENLY HARMONY

*"Where I am going, you cannot follow me now,
though you will follow later."* JOHN 13:36

A young man from my parish was traveling in Italy when the white smoke rose from the Vatican chimney. It was a vocations pilgrimage, and the group had stopped in Assisi to visit sites from St. Francis' life before making an abrupt change in their itinerary due to the conclave. They found themselves in St. Peter's Square when a man named Bergoglio came to the balcony. At first, my friend couldn't fully absorb it all. "Those moments were so full of ecstatic joy and uninhibited celebration alongside people from all over the world," he says. "It was definitely a glimpse of heaven." But as his friends commented on the coincidence that occurred that evening, he began to see something deeper at work. Maybe I should have mentioned that my friend's name is Francis. When the coincidence is that perfectly orchestrated, can it be anything other than God calling? Let's pray for vocations today.

FAMILY PRAYER

Parent: Lord, we are your children. Help us hear your voice
and discover the special work you want each of us to do.
All: We love you, Lord Jesus. Amen.

Pray silently to the Holy Spirit for guidance.

FAMILY ACTIVITY

Take a virtual trip with your kids to the Holy Land. Visit Google Earth or take a trip to your local library to show your kids the places in Jesus' life.

ISAIAH 50:4–9A » MATTHEW 26:14–25

I WISH...

The Lord GOD is my help, therefore I am not disgraced; I have set my face like flint, knowing that I shall not be put to shame. ISAIAH 50:7

Knowing that most of her students came from low-income families, Colorado teacher Kyle Schwartz wanted to understand her third graders better. She asked them to complete the following sentence: I wish my teacher knew—. The responses were heartbreaking. Maybe you've seen them on social media. One child said he didn't have any pencils at home to do his homework. Another said he missed his dad who'd been deported three years ago. The children didn't have to write their names, but many of them did anyway. Today, let's pray for kids who have no one to pray for them.

FAMILY PRAYER

Parent: Lord, we thank you for our family.

   All: Our hope is in the Lord.

Parent: With you at our side, Lord, we will run and not grow weary; walk and not grow faint.

   All: Our hope is in the Lord.

Parent: We will soar on eagle's wings. We ask this for our family and all families of the world.

   All: Our hope is in the Lord.

Bless everyone present, in your own way.

FAMILY ACTIVITY

If you haven't already, visit the Operation Rice Bowl website with your family to learn about how you can help the poor around the world. Go to www.crsricebowl.org.

EXODUS 12:1–8, 11–14 » 1 CORINTHIANS 11:23–26 » JOHN 13:1–15

BE CLEAN

*"If I, therefore, the master and teacher, have washed your feet,
you ought to wash one another's feet."* JOHN 13:14

My kids know the drill. They can play outside in the mud for as long
as they want, as long as they hose themselves off, come in through the
garage, and deposit dirty clothes directly in the washing machine. The
ritual has always served us well. The kids get to enjoy their beloved
mud, and I don't break my back cleaning up. Rituals are important
for practical and spiritual reasons, which is why it's good to introduce
children to tonight's Holy Thursday liturgy. After these weeks of serving others, they'll get to witness their pastor serve others by washing
parishioners' feet. Let's also pray today for children who don't have
access to clean water.

FAMILY PRAYER

Parent: Lord, many people are thirsty.

All: I thirst.

Parent: Many don't have clean water to drink.
Others search for living water.

All: I thirst.

Parent: Lord, you bring water and life to us all.

All: I thirst. Thank you, God. Amen.

Pray silently for victims of drought around the world.

FAMILY ACTIVITY

If you can't get to church tonight, read John 13:1–15, and have a foot-
washing ceremony at home. Be conscious of the millions of people
who don't have access to clean water, and use the water from your
ceremony to water plants.

Isaiah 52:13—53:12 » Hebrews 4:14–16; 5:7–9 » John 18:1—19:42

LOOKING UP

There they crucified him, and with him two others,
one on either side, with Jesus in the middle. John 19:18

After these long weeks of prayer, fasting, and almsgiving, Lent is nearly over. Today we contemplate Jesus suffering on the cross. We stand with Mary as she sees her good and beautiful boy, bloodied, tortured, and humiliated. Somehow our lenten experience doesn't seem that difficult. But it doesn't mean our fasting and almsgiving have no value. Exactly the opposite is true. Jesus has transformed everything we've done by his love and through his suffering. He has not missed our smallest sacrifices. Let's pray today for all young people who are in physical or mental pain. Let's ask Jesus to lift them up and care for them in his Father's compassionate name.

FAMILY PRAYER *(A Veneration of the Cross)*

Kneel before a cross, or hold one in your hands. Pass it slowly and reverently from person to person as you say the following prayer:
We see the cross that's made of wood; we remember Jesus, kind and good. Jesus on the cross is true; Jesus died for me and you.

Make the sign of the cross as you pass the cross to the next person.

FAMILY ACTIVITY
If you can't make Good Friday services, go outside for a few moments and look at the sky together, remembering Jesus' sacrifice. If you have a cross or crucifix, use the prayer above to venerate it.

Genesis 1:1—2:2 *or* 1:1, 26–31a » Genesis 22:1–18 *or* 22:1–2, 9a, 10–13, 15–18
Exodus 14:15–15:1 » Isaiah 54:5–14 » Isaiah 55:1–11
Baruch 3:9–15, 32—4:4 Ezekiel 36:16–17a, 18–28
Romans 6:3–11 » Luke 24:1–12

CALLED TO WORK

*But at daybreak on the first day of the week they took the spices
they had prepared and went to the tomb.* Luke 24:1

I bet they couldn't sleep. They'd been awake all night and now that it was daybreak, the women finally had something to do. They had a purpose. The anointing was for the body, but deep down, they knew it was for them. After all they had seen these past few days, they needed this. They needed to minister in some way, to heal something, even if it was a dead body. Each of us needs to heal and minister to others. Sure, that's a parent's role, but it's also a very basic human need. Lent has given us the chance to prepare the spices. Now it's time to go visit the empty tomb.

FAMILY PRAYER *(Based on the Exsultet Prayer of the Easter Vigil)*

Each person who is able can read a line.
Be glad, let earth be glad, as glory floods her,
ablaze with light from her eternal King,
let all corners of the earth be glad,
knowing the end to gloom and darkness is here. Amen.

Everyone shout, "Alleluia! Alleluia! Jesus is risen! Happy Easter!"

FAMILY ACTIVITY
If you're dyeing Easter eggs today, be sure to paint one a mottled gray or brown to represent the stone that was placed before Jesus' tomb. Talk to your children about how Easter eggs remind us of the new life that we have in Jesus.

TIME FOR CELEBRATING!

"He is not here." The tomb is empty. Jesus is risen. Let him be with you today in all your celebrations. Let his love pour into your heart and spill out and cover your family. Let your kids sing, shout, eat, dance, pray, play, and praise today. Bask in the light of Jesus' resurrection and the new life he promises you for the next fifty days of the Easter season. And celebrate his love all the days of your life. Alleluia! Alleluia!

Happy and blessed Easter to you! God bless your beautiful family!